TRADITIONAL LATIN MASS

A Pious Guide For Altar Server To Derive Fruits From The Tridentine Mass

Jesusa Echevarria
Paul Bryan Catolico
Bimby Macbs

COPYRIGHT @ 2023 TRADITIONAL LATIN MASS
A Pious Guide For Altar Server To Derive Fruits From The Tridentine Mass
By Jesusa Echevarria, Paul Bryan Catolico, Bimby Macbs

ISBN:
Hardbound-978-621-470-594-8
MOBI/KINDLE-978-621-470-595-5
Softbound/Paperback-978-621-470-596-2

Published by:
Poetry Planet Book Publishing House
Rosario, Pozorrubio, Pangasinan, Philippines
Contact Number: 09554960094
Email: maritesritumalta@gmail.com

Table Of Contents

Foreword

Nothing seems tiresome or painful when you are working for a Master who pays well; who rewards even a cup of cold water given for love of Him.

~St.Dominic Savio

Saint Dominic Savio is the patron saint of those who are falsely accused, delinquent juveniles, choirboys, and altar servers. He died at the age of 14, but even as a sickly and small child, his faith was towering and monumental. He endured extreme mortification, lived a pure and chaste life, had an intense love of the Holy Eucharist, and rendered spirited service in the Holy Mass as an altar server. His passionate words were "Death but not sin".

This book is written, firstly, to strengthen the virtues of chastity, obedience, and humility among altar servers; secondly, to be pleasing in serving in the Holy Mass through confession; and thirdly, for the avoidance of sin. As St. John "Don" Bosco (confessor and spiritual father of St. Dominic Savio) has stated, if you are serious about your soul, weekly confession and gaining fruits from the Sacrament of Penance is necessary.

This book is beneficial for those who will dedicate their lives to serving the Traditional Latin Mass and for the faithful who has no inkling about the dynamics, nature, and the Real Presence of Jesus during the Holy Mass.

BE HOLY, BE AN ALTAR SERVER

To be an Altar Server is a great privilege for Catholic boys. To be so chosen and be so close to Jesus for an hour during Mass is a favor from God. It must be done with reverence and awe of His Goodness and Greatness.

Today, the silence of the Holy Sacrifice of the Mass reverberates more than ever in the hearts of God's most faithful. But the beauty and meaning of the Tridentine Latin Mass are hidden from the naked, untutored, and skeptical eyes. We, as believers, must believe that in every movement, every gesture, and every word Jesus is there. All of heaven is there to adore God with us. And graces abound for us all present at Calvary once again.

~Yuhsa

A brief explanation of the Traditional Latin Mass.

This is the Mass of the Roman rite which has been celebrated throughout the world up until 1969. The Traditional Latin Mass is sometimes (although mistakenly) referred to as the Tridentine Mass, because the Roman Missal was codified by Pope Saint Pius V, at the specific request of the Fathers of the Council of Trent in the sixteenth century (the adjective 'Tridentine' is derived from the name Trent). It is important to recall, however, that what Pius V published in 1570 was a Missal based upon the continuous liturgical practice of the Church since the time of Pope Saint Gregory the Great in the sixth century.

The Traditional Latin Mass has sustained the Western Church for the last 1,500 years.

It is this Mass that has inspired all the great saints and martyrs of the Church and nourished the faith of countless generations of the faithful. It is the Mass that was taken by missionaries all over the world to win souls for Christ.

The Traditional Latin Mass is also called the Mass of the Roman Rite. After the Council of Trent, Pope Saint Pius V issued the Bull Quo Primum Tempore (1570) which promulgated the Roman Mass now codified for the first time in the Church's history.

The Bull also guaranteed the use of the Roman Rite in perpetuity and confirmed the traditional rites of various religious orders (such as the Dominicans) where these had been in use for at least 200 years.

Traditional Latin Mass, Priest, and Jesus Christ

Introduction

Why do teens want a Traditional Latin Mass?

The desire of teens and young people towards the Traditional Latin Mass is not motivated by influence but by an internal longing for beauty, silence, orthodoxy, and reverence in Holy Mass. Above all, the longing is the work of the Holy Ghost.

Beauty is the reflection of God, and young people are attracted to it. Silence allows young people to focus their thoughts on God, and reverence is intensified in the prayerful nature of the Holy Mass.

After Vatican II, almost only the older Filipino generation have experienced the Traditional Latin Mass. Spanish colonization had brought about the Catholic conversion of Filipinos. But after Vatican II, it is only mostly the aging Filipino generation who remember the Traditional Latin Mass. Alas, true Catholic Faith was lost to us, mainly because of the passage of time, and the absence of Catholic instruction, formation and practice.

Five hundred years ago, the first Holy Mass was in Latin, as documented by Padre Pedro de Valderrama. It was sadly abandoned and forgotten until a congregation of priests celebrated TLM again on these isles.

Now, in the 20th century, there is a vital need to uphold the Traditional Latin Mass to counter massive confusion, heresy, apostasy, modernism, and rationalization of sins. The Traditional Latin Mass is now gaining momentum. This is evident in the congregation of faithfuls, the families that pray the Mass together, and the passion and determination of every young man offering service to Jesus through the Holy Mass as altar servers.

Mass Of The Catechumens

In the "Mass Of The Catechumens" in the early church, the Catechumens are only allowed to attend the first part of the Mass. Catechumens are unbaptized people who yearned to be Catholic and under instruction, catechism, and training.

Preparation At The Foot Of The Altar

Priest At The Mass

When the Priest goes to the altar and begins to pray at the foot of the altar, the Priest makes the Sign of the Cross. In Traditional Latin Mass, the Sign of the Cross is reverently accomplished 52 times. This is the insignia of the bloody Sacrifice of the Cross which the Holy Mass embodies and renews. The Priest is reminding us of the significance of the Altar and the Holy Mass.

Jesus Christ

Jesus walks through Mount Olive, enters the Garden of Gethsemane, and prays.

Priest At The Mass

When the Priest says the Confiteor (I Confess), we must purify ourselves before placing ourselves in the Holy Presence of God. The Priest takes public avowal, appealing to God, with the Church Triumphant and Church Militants as his witnesses. All faithful in the Holy Mass accuse themselves and plead for God's mercy while seeking the intercession of the saints. The Church's absolution purifies and cleanses the soul.

Jesus Christ

Jesus falls on His face to the earth and sweats blood.

Priest At The Mass

The Priest kisses the altar in the middle where the relics of the Saints are enclosed.

Jesus Christ

Jesus is betrayed with a kiss.

The Priest At The Mass

When the Priest goes to the side of the epistle at the right side of the tabernacle, he makes the Sign of the Cross and reads the Introit.

Jesus Christ

Jesus Christ is bound as a prisoner and led to Annas.

The Priest At The Mass

When the Priest reads the Introit.

Jesus Christ

Jesus Christ is falsely accused by Annas and blasphemed severely.

The Priest At The Mass

He goes to the middle of the Altar and recites "Kyrie" which means "Lord Have Mercy." It is the only part of the Holy Mass that is written in Greek. If it is written in Latin, it will lose its original meaning.

Jesus Christ

Jesus is brought to Caiaphas and denied by St. Peter three times.

Priest At The Mass

The Priest kisses the altar, turns towards people, and says "Dominus Vobiscum" (The Lord be with you) with a downcast eye. The faithful respond "Et cum spiritu tuo" (And with thy spirit). This is repeated several times in the Traditional Latin Mass, an intimate expression of the Priest and faithful that should be united in offering the Sacrifice.

Jesus Christ

Jesus looks at Peter and converts him.

Priest At The Mass

At Gloria, the priest stands at the center of the altar, extends, and then joins his hands and makes a slight bow. Gloria is omitted when the priest's vestments are black or violet (Lent, Advent, and Masses for the dead).

Jesus Christ

Angels announced the birth of our Lord Jesus Christ.

Priest At The Mass

Priest goes to the Missal and reads the Collects and the Epistle.

Jesus Christ

Jesus Christ is brought to Pontius Pilate.

Priest At The Mass

At the "Munda cor meum," The Missal is moved to the Gospel side (to the left of the Tabernacle) while the Priest bows at the middle of the altar with his hands joined. With the Priest, we sign our forehead with the Cross as a manifestation of our belief in the Gospel; we cross our lips, as this depicts our respect for the Gospel in speech; and we mark our heart with the Cross to illustrate our love for it.

Jesus Christ

He was brought into Herod's court and was blatantly mocked. Then Jesus Christ was sent back by Herod to Pontius Pilate.

Priest At The Mass

Then the Priest returns to the middle of the Altar and recites the Creed. Creed is the solemn and public profession of our faith. It was drawn up from a General Council of Nicea in 325 that condemned heretics who denied Jesus Christ and the Holy Ghost.

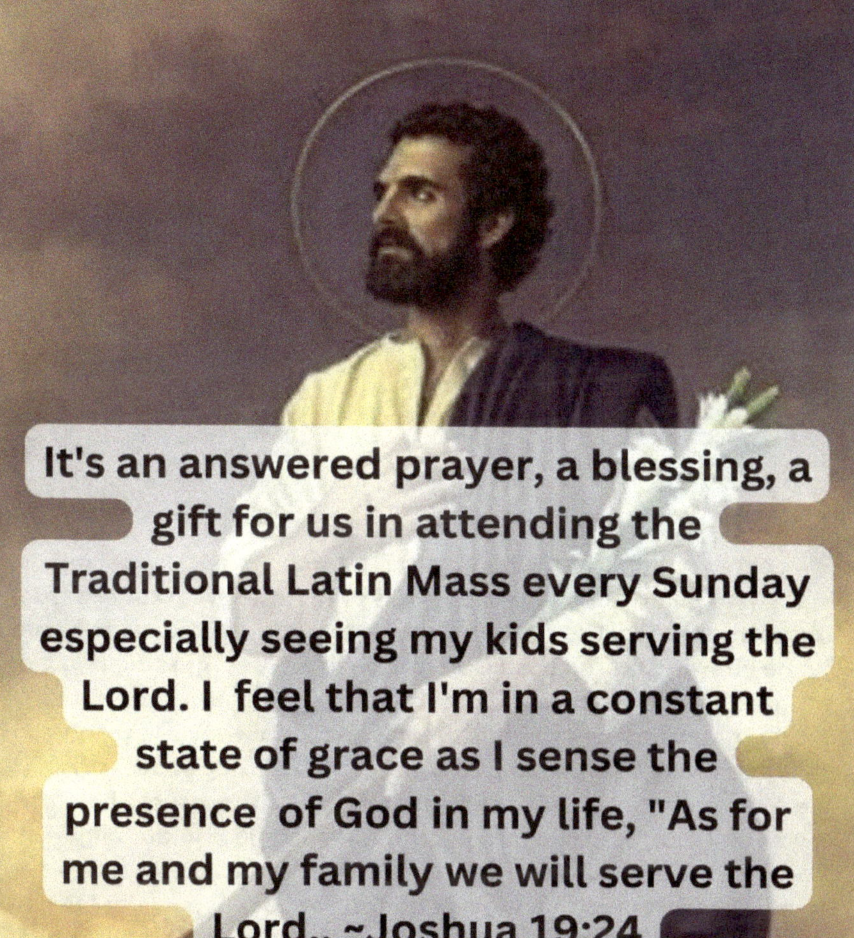

It's an answered prayer, a blessing, a gift for us in attending the Traditional Latin Mass every Sunday especially seeing my kids serving the Lord. I feel that I'm in a constant state of grace as I sense the presence of God in my life, "As for me and my family we will serve the Lord.. ~Joshua 19:24
Johnson Anthony Uy
ALTAR SERVER'S FATHER

A parent of children who do altar service is a great privilege because their willingness to serve is one of the greatest rewards for us as parents. The only goal we have accomplished is to serve the church and the Lord God has been a great blessing to us. Since our children went to church and served as altar servers, many things have happened such as trials but they are resolved, and many blessings have come that were not expected.
We prayed that our children could enter as altar servers because first of all, our Catholic faith would be restored and our children would be kept away from bad influence, especially in today's times. Parents need to have a good foundation, especially faith in God in the traditional Latin Mass and to guide their children properly so that they can be a good example to today's youth. In this way, God-fearing children can be properly raised.

Maureen J. Uy
Mother of 3 Altar Servers

Mass Of The Faithful

At this point, in the ancient Church, the catechumens were then excluded from the rest of the Mass and only the baptized Faithful could remain. (Reverent Catholic Mass)

Priest At The Mass

The Priest unveils the Chalice.

Jesus Christ

Jesus is divested of His garments.

Priest At The Mass

The Offertory

Jesus Christ

Jesus Christ is scourged at the pillar.

Priest At The Mass

The Priest covers the Chalice with a pall.

Jesus Christ

Jesus is crowned with thorns.

Priest At The Mass

The Priest washes his hand at the Epistle side of the altar.

Jesus Christ

Pontius Pilate washes his hand and declares "I am innocent of the blood of this person.

Priest At The Mass

The Priest turns toward the faithful and says "Orate Frates" (Pray for brethren).

Jesus Christ

Pilate said to people "Behold this man" referring to our Lord Jesus Christ.

Priest At The Mass

The Preface is a way to bestow thanks to God the Father through our Lord Jesus Christ in union with all the heavenly spirits.

Jesus Christ

Jesus is condemned to die and they freed Barabas.

Priest At The Mass

The Priest joins hands and says "Sanctus" The bell rang three times. At High Mass, everyone kneels after singing.

Jesus Christ

It is the triumphal hymn of the angel. It is addressed to the three Divine Persons.

Canon Of The Mass

31

Priest At The Mass

At the memento for the living…

Jesus Christ

Jesus bears His Cross.

Priest At The Mass

At the Hanc Igitur when the priest holds his hands over the chalice.

Jesus Christ

Jesus Christ comforts the women who mourn in Jerusalem.

Priest At The Mass

The Priest signs the population.

Jesus Christ

Jesus Christ is nailed on the Cross.

Priest At The Mass

The Priest elevates the Host.

Jesus Christ

The cross is lifted and Jesus sees His mother, the Blessed Virgin Mary kneeling.

When servers lift the chasuble during the elevation of the Host, it is a depiction of the woman suffering from hemorrhage who touches the hem of Jesus' cloth and was healed.

Priest At The Mass

Elevation of the Chalice.

Jesus Christ

Jesus' blood flows from His wounds.

Priest At The Mass

The Memento for the dead.

Jesus Christ

Jesus prays for the world.

Priest At The Mass

At Nobis Quoque Peccatoribus.

Jesus Christ

The thief is converted.

Priest At The Mass

The Priest prostrates himself before the Host and Chalice.

Jesus Christ

Jesus Christ cries out "I thirst".

Priest At The Mass

Pater Noster (The Lord's Prayer)

Jesus Christ

Jesus speaks the 7 Last words at the Cross.

Priest At The Mass

The breaking of the Host.

Jesus Christ

Jesus dies on the Cross.

Priest At The Mass

The Priest puts a piece of Host in the Chalice

Jesus Christ

The soul of Jesus descends into Hell (Abraham's Bosom). It is called the harrowing of hell.

Priest At The Mass

Agnus Dei

Jesus Christ

Many of those who were present in the Crucifixion were converted. Jesus Christ was acknowledged as the Son Of God by the witnesses of the Crucifixion.

Priest At The Mass

The Holy Communion.

Jesus Christ

Jesus Christ was buried and His body is laid in the sepulcher.

Priest At The Mass

The Ablution

Jesus Christ

Jesus Christ's body is anointed in the sepulcher.

Priest At The Mass

After Communion, the priest cleanses and prepares the chalice again. He turns to the people, and says "Dominus vobiscum." Then he reads the communion and post-communion prayers.

Jesus Christ

Jesus Christ, our Lord rises from the dead. He appears to His mother and His disciples, and he teaches them for 40 days. He triumphs over death with His resurrection.

Priest At The Mass

Turns to the people and says the last "Dominus vobiscum." Then he says "Ite, missa est."

Jesus Christ

Jesus bids farewell to His disciples. He commissions the apostles to preach the gospel to the whole world, and He ascends into heaven.

Priest At The Mass

The Priest gives the final blessing to the faithful. The prayer that comes after the dismissal is a petition to God that the sacrifice will be beneficial and useful for the priest and the faithful.

Jesus Christ

God sends down the Holy Ghost on Pentecost.

Priest At The Mass

The Priest reads the gospel of St. John.

Jesus Christ

In the last gospel, St. John proclaims that Jesus Christ is the Incarnation of the Son Of God, the Word made Flesh, the source of life on earth.

For Low Mass

Ave Maria, Salve Regina, and St. Michael are the prayers that are being said after the Holy Mass.

"There are a few things I noticed as I entered the Immaculate Conception Church: it is incredibly quiet inside, the mass is said in Latin, and the altar is different from the altars in other parishes. When I went to mass for the first time, I immediately realized that it was a Traditional Latin Mass in the 9th grade, we learned about traditional mass in which the priest always faces the altar rather than the people. I've felt blessed by God ever since I began serving in the Traditional Latin Mass, and I find happiness in it. I also adore serving in Traditional Latin Mass."

~Joseph, 18 years old, Altar Server

My experience as Altar Server is not bad, when I kneel for a long time, I think of good thoughts and keep my patience. It is tiring because the longer I stand, my legs hurt, so I keep my focus on the Priest and Jesus on the altar.

~Japheth, 12 years old, Altar Server

Participating in the Holy Mass has been one of the most wonderful and rewarding experiences I've ever had. The people in the church, including our priest, are the nicest and most genuine people I've ever met, and I feel like I'm part of a larger family that is all about serving the people and our Lord God.

As an altar server who has experienced both the modern and Traditional Latin Mass, I can attest to the unique and profound nature of these ancient forms of liturgy. During the Traditional Latin Mass, the priest faces the altar, and the Latin language is predominantly used, which adds to the sense of solemnity and reverence.

The difference can be seen and felt because the people truly participate in every response and listen attentively to the priest during the Mass and Catechism (after the Mass). During these moments, you can sense the solemnity and peace in the church.

It's typical to experience and encounter a sense of belongingness and familiarity when participating in a Holy Mass, but for me, that sentiment can be particularly profound. Such is the case for those who have attended the Traditional Latin Mass for the first time. Despite being a new experience, I have this excitement like coming home, as if it were a part of one's soul all along. All fears and anxieties fade away in the quiet reverence of the ancient language and ritual, allowing one to immerse oneself fully in the beauty and wonder of the liturgy.

~Benedict, 15, Altar Server

"At first I was not so used to it but now I feel great that I am one of the servers that Fr. Becher trusts during mass. The Traditional Latin Mass taught us many prayers, how to confess and why it is important. I learned how to pray The Holy Rosary and most of all, I had my first communion during Christmas Eve's High mass which made me and my mommy very happy. When I am at the altar, I feel very blessed knowing that I am so close to all the angels as they watch me serve for our Lord Jesus Christ.

- Luke, 10 years old, Altar Server

"I love The Traditional Mass. At first, I was confused and filled with questions about it because I used to go to New Mass but later on, I realized that The Latin Mass is the first mass ever taught since the time of Jesus Christ. I have learned so many things from our Catechism and one thing I value the most is going to confessions. It gives me a good feeling to receive Jesus Christ knowing that I have done my penance. I have learned to love The Traditional Latin Mass, I feel proud and happy that I can serve it each time and give value to the sacrifice that the Lord Jesus Christ had suffered to save us from our sins."
~Travis, 11 years old, Altar Server

"When I attended the Traditional Latin Mass for the first time, I didn't fully understand it. The entry of the Priest was so quiet as he goes to the altar, facing the Tabernacle. I was praying along but honestly, I didn't know how to respond or when to do it, or what's next. It was confusing to me in the beginning. Later then, I knew that I attended a Low Mass which I now truly appreciate. I love basking in the moment of the solemnity that I've experienced from the moment the Priest ascends to the foot of the Altar and stands before the throne of grace of God leading and preparing the people to come, worship and glorify Him. When the Priest says The

Confiteor, it reminded me of my life as a sinner, unworthy but wanting to be with God. Although I didn't understand the Latin Mass even at the beginning, I kept going and I was drawn to it. In the Novus Ordo, I feel so required to respond but in the Latin Mass, I can be quiet and reflect on what the Priest is doing as he leads us back to the sacrifice of our Lord. I cannot explain well in words but I would say I can see the reverence and honor that the servers and The Priest are giving the Lord, in the sacred scriptures, in genuflection, signing of the cross, and especially in the Eucharist. I suppose that is why we call it the mystery of our faith. I kept on returning because as for me, I am truly basking on God's Divine Presence and receiving The Lord Jesus Christ more reverently in the Holy Communion, kneeling and on the tongue. Furthermore, Traditional Catholicism has changed me little by little because of the reminders of the Traditional Priest that as Catholics we must always avail the sacraments to receive the graces from the Lord. My experience is so humbling and I'm continually learning. Ultimately, indeed, the Traditional Latin Mass is simple, profound, and a beautiful treasure."

~Michelle, Traditional Latin Mass faithful

Lord help me

to remember

that nothing

is going to happen

to me today

that You and I

together can't handle.

Amen.

(Before Mass)

Oh Jesus, my King, and Lord,
by the grace of the heavenly Father
and the power of the Holy Spirit,
guide me in all righteousness
as I serve You today at the Altar
so I may be always worthy of Your presence.
If I happen to make an error,
may it be a lesson
so my service will be perfect tomorrow.
Jesus, I love you with all my heart.

Amen.

Altar Server Prayer

(After Mass)

Lord Jesus,
thank you for the opportunity
to serve You during the Holy Mass.
In Your Sacred Presence,
my heart is filled with joy and peace.
May Your Spirit always guide me
so I may grow in Your love
by the grace of the Heavenly Father.

Amen.

Reflections on Attending Traditional Latin Mass

The Traditional Latin Mass is a holy liturgy that has been celebrated for hundreds of years, and which persists to attract faithful Catholics to this day. As a faithful attendee of the Traditional Latin Mass, I can vouch for the profound influence it has had on my spiritual journey. The holiness, solemnity, reverence, and devotion that are present in this form of adoration and worship bring forth a sense of astonishment for the mystery of God and it engraved in me virtues such as humility, obedience, and the love of Jesus Christ.

One of the most notable aspects of the Traditional Latin Mass is the stillness and the silence that envelops the congregation. Whereas in more modern forms of liturgy, there may be an incredible deal of noise and unrest, in the Latin Mass there is a sense of serenity that entitles one to concentrate on the prayers, the rubrics, and the gesture of the server and the priest. This quietness enables one to develop an atmosphere of reverence, where one can more efficiently enter into a state of prayerful reflection and contemplation.

In complement to the silence, the magnificence of the Traditional Latin Mass is also an attraction for many of the young faithful. The Gregorian chant, the detailed vestments of the priest, and the art and architecture of the church itself – all contributed to the sense of transcendence that is present in this form of worship. The beauty of the Latin Mass is not simply superficial but communicates the inner beauty of the soul and its yearning for God.

Furthermore, the rigid abidance to rubrics and gestures in the Traditional Latin Mass highlights the importance of liturgical tradition as a vehicle for a nourishing faith. Every rubric, every word, and every gesture has a deep symbolic purpose and enables us to bind the faithful to the rich tradition of Catholic liturgy that has been handed down through the ages. In this way, the Traditional Latin Mass operates as a living link to the ancient roots of Christianity, and a testimony to its enduring relevance.

Nevertheless conceivably most significantly, the Traditional Latin Mass carries us closer to our divine God. As Catholics, we believe that the bread and wine consecrated during the Mass truly become the real body and blood of our Lord Jesus Christ, and that in receiving Communion we are in fellowship with Him. In the Traditional Latin Mass, this mystery is created even more palpable through the holiness of the priest who celebrates it. The solemnity of the ritual, the reverence of the congregation, and the beauty of the liturgy all serve to make us more conscious of the real presence of Jesus in the Eucharist.

Likewise, the benefits of the Traditional Latin Mass extend beyond the Mass itself. For example, the Sacrament of Confession is an integral part of this form of worship and is available before, during, and after the Mass. As such, the faithful have more opportunities to be in the state of grace and to receive the fullness of God's grace.

Undoubtedly, my experience with the Traditional Latin Mass has been transformative, propelling me toward the virtues that God yearns for us all. Through the solemnity, beauty, reverence, and real presence of Jesus, I have established joy, humility, and obedience to God's will. And I have also caught a glimpse of the conversion that this form of adoration can bring to others as well.

For instance, I have personally carried many faithful to the Traditional Latin Mass, and have witnessed how it has transformed their lives. One family in particular was restored by serving Jesus in this holy Mass; forgiveness took place and many of their prayers were responded. In this way, the Traditional Latin Mass administers as an agent of evangelization, bringing souls closer to Christ and aiding to build up the Kingdom of God.

The Traditional Latin Mass is the mass of the saints, its sanctity of a person and it is like a saint-making machine that will truly transform a person if he is sensitive and cooperative to the prompting of the Holy Ghost, and the divine will of God.

The Traditional Latin Mass is an affluent and powerful form of Catholic adoration and worship, one that has made the lives of countless faithful throughout the ages. Its intenseness on silence, beauty, rubrics, and gestures fosters an environment of reverence and belief and works for the faithful to attach more deeply to the mystery of God. I firmly encourage all Catholics to partake in Traditional Latin Mass, as it has much to bestow to those who seek to thrive in their faith and draw closer to God.

Bimby, Faithful to Traditional Latin Mass

Guide In Serving Traditional Latin Mass

The Traditional Latin Mass, also known as the Extraordinary Form of the Roman Rite, is the liturgical form of the Roman Catholic Church that was solely embraced before the Second Vatican Council and still lingering until the present. This form of liturgy has earned interest in contemporary years among young Catholics who pursue an unsurpassed traditional and reverential liturgy. In this composition, we will talk about how to serve as an altar server properly in the Traditional Latin Mass.

Before delving into the specifics of serving in the Extraordinary Form, it is significant to figure out the function of the altar server in the Mass. The altar server is a layperson who attends to the priest during the celebration of the Mass. The server's function is to assist prepare the liturgical vessels, carry the missal and other items, and support the priest with any other necessities.

When you are serving as a server in the Traditional Latin Mass, there are some key things to uphold in mind to make sure that the Mass is celebrated with proper reverence and solemnity.

First and foremost, the server must be a baptized male Catholic, a communicant, and must always be in a state of grace while serving in the Holy Mass. An altar server must be pleasing to God by going to Confession twice monthly. He must be pleasing to God.

He must be properly attired. This includes wearing a cassock and surplice, and in some cases, a cotta or mozzetta. The cassock is a long, black garment that covers the server's body, and the surplice is a white garment worn over the cassock. The cotta and mozzetta are optional garments worn over the surplice.

When readying for the Mass, the server must come earlier to make certain that everything is in order. This comprises making sure that the altar is appropriately set up with the proper liturgical vessels and candles, and that the server's things, such as the missal and thurible, are prepared for use. It is also essential for the server to go over their responsibilities with the priest or master of ceremonies to make sure that they know precisely what is counted on them.

During the Mass, the server must be prudent and focused on their responsibilities. They should change positions with purpose and precision, and try to minimize any undue noise or action. When accepting or holding liturgical vessels, the server should use both hands and handle them with care and reverence.

One of the most vital duties of the server during the Traditional Latin Mass is making the responses. The Latin responses are an integral part of the Mass, and the server's clear and confident responses benefit to produce a reverential atmosphere. To guarantee that responses are put together accurately, the server must practice them beforehand and pay close concentration to the priest as he says the prayers.

Another essential aspect of serving at the Traditional Latin Mass is the proper use of incense. Incense is utilized during the Mass to signify the prayers of the faithful ascending to heaven. The server should be knowledgeable about the correct use of the thurible, including how to light and extinguish it, how to load it with incense, and how to swing it during the Mass.

Finally, the server must be conscious of their position during the Mass, and confirm that they are standing or sitting in the proper place at the proper time. This includes knowing when to step forward to hand the priest liturgical vessels when to kneel, and when to shift to distinct parts of the altar.

In summation, serving as an altar server in the Traditional Latin Mass is a tremendous privilege and responsibility. The server's function is necessary for assisting the priest celebrate the Mass with reverence and dignity. By obeying the guidelines outlined above, the server can assure that they are fulfilling their function with acceptable reverence and solemnity, and chipping into the beauty of the Traditional Latin form of the Mass.

Afterword

Altar Servers, more commonly known as altar boys, are children or teenagers who assist a priest during Mass. The term comes from the Latin word "ministry" which means "to serve." Their role is recognized by the Conciliar Constitution as an integral part of the liturgic office. As such, it demands conduct and behavior from those who serve that are in keeping with it.

Altar Servers must follow the example of Jesus, who did not hesitate to place himself wholly for humanity's service and even sacrificed himself. Not only during services, but also throughout everyday life, Altar Servers must live by following His example of love, generosity, commitment, and precision.

Altar Servers are Jesus' 'friends,' usually young people full of enthusiasm and willingness to take part in the activities of the Church by offering their contributions of love and devotion.

In the history of the Church, there have been many characters who could represent the ideal model for Altar Servers, like Saint Tarcisius, who lived in the era of the first Christian communities in Rome and was killed by his pagan peers because he had made himself available to carry the Blessed Sacrament to Christian prisoners. Or, Saint Dominic Savio, who had Saint John Bosco as a teacher and guide, and devoted his (unfortunately short) life to his brothers and the community.

I can't do big things, but I want everything to be for
the glory of God.

St. Dominic Savio

The Authors

Jesusa Angela Echevarria is a cradle Catholic who was raised and schooled with traditional values. As the world turned modern, she navigated life by working in computer programming, business management, and public education. Teaching elementary and college students in the Philippines and the US inspired her advocacy for reading. It is now tied with her love for catechism and charity for the lost and the little.

It is out of God's utmost love for her that she learned about the Traditional Latin Mass from her fellow faithful. Today, by God's Grace, her soul is a work in progress for holiness. She has fully and happily returned to tradition, as everyone ought to. She is now leading the music ministry in the church, writing for children, and depending on Heaven for her every need and want. She sometimes identifies with St. Joan of Arc, and at times relates with St. John "Don" Bosco.

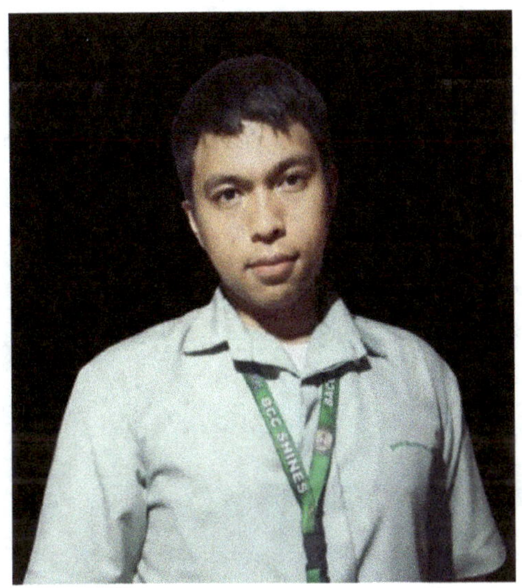

Paul Bryan Catolico is presently a Traditional Latin Mass Server at Immaculate Conception Roman Catholic Church -SSPX. He is a graduating college student. He is a Student Governor.

He shows zeal in serving the Holy Mass. He mentored and taught young boys the proper rubrics of the Tridentine Mass.

He is inspired by the work of saints which makes him fall in love with the Traditional Latin Mass. His spiritual journey is influenced by St. Alphonsus Maria Ligouri, St. Bonaventure, and Pius X.

Bimby Macbs is a Registered Nurse in the Philippines and has worked as an Academe Marketing and Sales Specialist.

He will be receiving his Doctor in Literature this April of 2023

He decides to discontinue his job and focus on freelance writing, catechism, and evangelization. He is a seminar lecturer, and career coach, conducting career orientation with students in secondary education in preparation for their college program.

He has training in the human temperament, love languages, and psycho-spiritual integration.

Bibliography

~The Holy Sacrifice Of The Mass
Photo by Junereybayla on Flickr. A painting inside the Chapel Of St. Benedict's Monastery, in Corte, Carmen, Cebu City, Philippines.

~Brief Explanation Of Traditional Latin Mass (SSPX website)

~ Traditional Latin Mass Photo

~Photos of Altar Server, Priest, and Jesus Pinterest (Zazzle)

~First Mass in the Philippines, Artnet, Pinterest

~ Altar Server Prayers
https://www.catholic.org/prayers/prayer.php?p=1128

~ Epilogue (Altar Server)
   Holy Art Blog

Grosse, C. (2018). How to Serve at a Traditional Latin Mass. Seton Magazine. Retrieved from https://www.setonmagazine.com/latest-articles/how-to-serve-at-a-traditional-latin-mass.

https://catolicoon.wordpress.com/missa-tridentina/